FAIR BEAR
Copyright © 2024 by Nicoleta Taylor

Hardcover ISBN: 978-1-962570-89-3
Paperback ISBN: 978-1-962570-90-9
eBook ISBN: 978-1-962570-91-6
Library of Congress Control Number: 2024920544

Written and designed by Nicoleta Taylor.
Illustrations generated with AI using Copilot.

amazon.com/author/nicoletataylor
nicoletataylor.com

Published in the United States by Spotlight Publishing House ™
spotlightpublishinghouse.com

Nicoleta Taylor's

# FAIR BEAR

A book that grows with you!

FAIR BEAR

## "This is a book that grows with you!"

Why, you ask? Well, let me tell you!

🐾 At first, it's all about the enchanting poem – a delightful, easy-to-remember rhyme that introduces you to all kinds of bears at a very early age. You'll find yourself captivated by them, falling in love with each furry friend.

🐾 But as you grow, so do your questions! You'll start asking "WHY?" a lot. Why is one bear's fur white while another's is brown? Why are they called bears? Why are there only eight of them? Why do they hibernate?

🐾 Whether you're snuggled up with a loved one who's reading the book to you, or you've started reading it on your own, fear not! At the end of this magical journey, you'll discover a treasure trove of answers to satisfy all your curious "whys." It's like having a charming bear guide who's ready to walk you through everything you want to know.

🐾 So dive in and let the adventure begin! This is more than just a book – it's a companion that will grow with you, sparking your imagination and answering your questions every step of the way!

A

black

bear,

a brown bear,
yes,
some call it
grizzly bear,

don't forget
the polar bear,
all wrapped up
in long white hair.
This is what
(s)he's born to wear!

# A
# spectacled
# Andean
# bear,

a shaggy
and fun
sloth
bear,

a

sun

bear,

a
moon
bear,

and,

of course,

a

panda

bear,

precious like
my teddy bear
sitting on
my little chair.
Wait,
is this
a fair bear?

(S)he is fair.
Please,
don't stare
when you see
that golden hair!

Ask
my bear
on my chair!

Yes,
it's rare,
says the bear,
calmly sitting
on the chair.

If you care,
any hair
looks perfect
on any bear,
if it's what
(s)he's born to wear.
Just think of
a spirit bear!

What
a thoughtful
teddy bear
with the cutest
fair hair
sitting on
my little chair!

I love this
and
have to share!

# Bear-ly Exploring:
# Discover the World of Bears
# with Fun and Facts!

🐾 Bears are amazing creatures, my friend!

🐾 **Did you know** that bears belong to a special family called Ursidae? This family is one of nine families in a cool group called "doglike" animals, or Caniformia. And guess what? Bears' closest living relatives are like their animal cousins—the pinnipeds (like seals and sea lions), canids (like dogs and foxes), and musteloids (think of cute weasels and otters). It's like bears have their own special branch on the family tree!

🐾 **Did you know** that there are only eight kinds of bears around today? These cool bears live in lots of different places in the Northern Hemisphere and a bit in the Southern Hemisphere too—on continents like North America, South America, and Eurasia (Europe and Asia). They are like the superheroes of the animal kingdom!

**Did you know** that a bear is a special kind of animal called a mammal? Let me tell you why it's so cool! Because they are a bit like us humans. Bear moms give birth to bear babies, and here's the best part: mammals, including bears, drink milk when they're babies! And not just that. Bears walk flat on their feet like us humans! And they eat just like humans, except that they don't cook! The polar bears love munching on meat, others like the giant panda prefer chomping on plants, and the rest of the bear gang is omnivore. That means they eat a bit of everything!

**Did you know** the word "bear" has a super interesting story? Some language detectives think the word "bear" is from a very old word that means "wild animal." The story goes like this: a long time ago, our friends from the proto-Germanic tribes had a word for bear, but they got a bit scared. They thought if they said the bear's real name, the bear might magically appear! So, they came up with a secret code and replaced the original word with a new one. Sneaky, right? It's like having a secret password for a magical creature!

**Did you know** that in the winter, some bears take a super long nap called hibernation? That is up to a whopping 100 days! When it's time for a snooze, bears find cozy spots like caves or logs to rest. Imagine having such a long and cozy sleepover in your own bear den!

**Did you know** that up in the night sky, there are two amazing groups of stars that look like bears? They're called Ursa Major and Ursa Minor, which means the great bear and the little bear. It's like finding bear-shaped puzzle pieces in the stars! And wait, there's a star nearby called Arcturus, the guardian of the bears. How cool is that? It's like having a cosmic bedtime story with bears and a star guardian!

**Did you know** that some bears are listed as vulnerable or endangered? This means we need to look out for them. We've put rules in place to protect bears, and make sure our bear buddies stay safe and happy in the wild. Let's be bear heroes together and keep our furry friends smiling!

Say hello to the **black bear**, also known as the American black bear!

This furry friend is the smallest bear in the forests of North America. Now, don't let the name fool you—these bears can be more than just black. Some of them can be brown or even blond! Nature sure loves to add a splash of color to these playful bears.

Meet the **brown bear**, a big bear that calls the forests across Eurasia and North America its home! In North America, it goes by the name grizzly bear, and on the Kodiak Islands of Alaska, it's known as the Kodiak bear. These bears are like nature's giants, exploring the wild and showing off different names depending on where they roam!

Greet the **polar bear**, a big and snowy white bear that calls the Arctic Circle its chilly home!

This bear loves to wander across the sea ice, enjoying the frosty views. Guess what? It's like a cousin to the brown bear, two bears from the same family with their own unique styles. The polar bear is the biggest of them all, like the king of the icy world!

Get to know the **Andean bear**, also known as the spectacled bear, Andean short-faced bear, or mountain bear!

This mid-sized bear loves hanging out in the Andes Mountains in western South America. Now, here's the cool part: it's a dark brown bear that wears special beige spectacle markings on its face and chest. It's like this bear has its very own stylish glasses!

Say hi to the **sloth bear**, a cool mid-sized bear with shaggy black fur and long, sickle-shaped claws! These bears love hanging out in the forests of India, having their own adventure. Guess what? They're also known as "labiated bears" because of their long lower lip, which they use like a super-hero tool for slurping up insects. It's like having their very own built-in straw!

Here is the **sun bear**, living happily in the tropical forests of Southeast Asia!

This little bear loves to snuggle up for lots of naps, whether it's high up in the trees or basking in the warm sun. With jet-black fur and a crescent moon patch on its chest, it's like nature gave it a special outfit! And you know what makes it even more special? It's the smallest bear of them all!

It's time to meet the Asian black bear, also known as the Asiatic black bear, **moon bear**, and white-chested bear!

This medium-sized bear is like a forest explorer, living in the magical lands of the Himalayas, the Korean Peninsula, and the islands of Japan and Taiwan. **It's got a distinct whitish patch on its chest, like a cozy badge of honor!**

Wave and say hello to the **panda bear**, also known as the giant panda, or just the panda!

This mid-sized bear is like a furry fashion icon with its bold black-and-white coat and a cute, round body. Guess where it loves to hang out? In the bamboo forests of China, munching on delicious bamboo shoots. It's like the panda has its very own black-and-white superhero costume!

Presenting the **spirit bear**, also known as the Kermode bear!

This bear is extraordinary because it's an incredibly rare white-coated American black bear found in the forests of British Columbia, Canada. And here's the magical part – it's not just rare; it's like a VIP in the culture of the indigenous people of the area. Imagine having a bear with a touch of enchantment!

And finally, say hello to Nicoleta Taylor's **fair bear**, a sweet teddy bear that visited her in a dream!

This caring bear is here to invite young minds on a magical journey through the wonders of nature's diversity, all wrapped up in playful and easy-to-remember poems. Stay tuned because, from this enchanting book about bears, more stories about the fair bear's family and friends are on the way!

Can you name all these bears?

FAIR BEAR'S CHALLENGE

# Nicoleta Taylor's Story

Once upon a time, in a charming Transylvanian village in Romania, lived a quiet little girl named Nicoleta. She loved reading and writing, and at just 14 years old, she won a poetry contest, becoming the youngest poet to receive that special prize.

As Nicoleta grew older, her talent for writing shone brighter. She won awards for language and literature, showing everyone that her words were like magic. Then, in her forties, she embarked on a grand adventure, moving to a sunny land called Phoenix in Arizona, USA. Her name became Nicoleta Taylor, connecting her Romanian past with her new American present.

Nicoleta's story is filled with the magic of two worlds coming together. On Earth Day in 2022, one of her dreams came true: she wrote a book of poetry called *Terrans: To MotherShip Terra's Stewards, with Love*, all about love for our planet, spirituality, and science fiction. But that's not all! She continues to write, with more books published and more in the making.

Nicoleta is also a language wizard! She translates and interprets between Romanian and English and teaches American students about Romanian language and culture. She even helps make the Duolingo app more magical with her linguistic skills.

And so, the amazing tale of Nicoleta, a talented writer, language wizard, and a friend to our beautiful planet, continues. The end!

If you loved our book, get ready for even more fun stories about our furry family and friends! Who's your favorite furry friend, and why do you love them? Email us at nicoleta.taylor@yahoo.com, and your pick might be in our next adventure!

Check out Nicoleta Taylor's books for adults and children at
amazon.com/author/nicoletataylor

Subscribe to her blog at
nicoletataylor.com

www.ingramcontent.com/pod-product-compliance
Lightning Source LLC
Chambersburg PA
CBHW042342030426
42335CB00030B/3436